I0201366

From

"Who Am I?"

To

"Who I Am!"

Shirley Cochran

Shirley Cochran

Published in the United States of America

by

GLORIFIED PUBLISHING
PO Box 8004
The Woodlands, TX 77387
www.GlorifiedPublishing.com

All scripture is taken from
The Holy Bible, New King James Version
Copyright 1982 by Thomas Nelson, Inc.

Copyright © 2017 Shirley Cochran

All rights reserved.

ISBN: **978-1-946106-33-9**

DEDICATION

To my three sons:

If I could live my life over knowing what I do now, I would have done a better job as a Mother. But since I can't, I have been told that I have a story to tell. Jesus has shown me what true Love is, so I pray you will accept my story of *Who Am I to Who I Am.*

Shirley Cochran

CONTENTS

Shirley Cochran

ACKNOWLEDGMENTS

This is dedicated to so many people that God has sent!

It has been an incredible journey, beginning with the signs from Him; to encouraging words from supporters; all the way to the finances at the end.

I haven't named names for a reason. I don't want to leave anyone out, so if I were to name names, I'm afraid I would. I can't thank you all enough.

You know who you are.

This has truly been a roller coaster ride. It's been up and down; No, Yes, Write! Put it away; Write, Put it away; Back and Forth, again and again. But now it's over. The Book has been written and by the time you see this, it will be published.

I thank my heavenly Father, Jesus Christ and the Holy Spirit, Who has worked in and through me.

The dots have all been connected now.

Shirley Cochran

INTRODUCTION

This book is about finding your identity, even though you think you know who you are in Christ. God knew me before I was in my Mother's womb, according to Jeremiah 1:5. I might have been a surprise to my parents, but I was no surprise to God.

This is my true story of going From *Who Am I* to *Who I Am*. I have no doubt there will be a lot of people who can relate with my story. People who weren't raised in Godly homes. Nothing is made up. Even when I didn't know God then, I can look back now and know He was there all the time, and that what He has done for me, He will do for others.

I Give God All The Glory!

Several times I have been told that I have a book in me. Being a bible study teacher, I just figured, "Yes, I have *The Book* in me." But at a retreat in Houston, Texas, Melody

Barker said, "There is someone here that needs to get your book going." God spoke to me and said "Yes that's you." He gave me the title right there. I spoke to Melody what happened. She later had me stand up, and asked the room to stretch their hands towards me to pray for me to get my Book going.

So, here goes!

1 FIRST ENCOUNTER

Growing up, I was never really special to anyone. Not to my Parents, or even in school. It seemed 'Rejection' was my middle name. It was either my best friend or it was my shadow, because it was always hanging around me.

I never had a close relationship with anyone. I never had a best friend. Growing up, it seems like someone was always fighting - my parents or my sisters and brothers. It was always them with each other or with me in the middle.

I was raised in an alcoholic dysfunctional family. When I was seven years old, we lived in Tooele, Utah. We took a vacation to California to see my mother's side of the family.

At a family reunion, where everyone was partying, one Aunt, the only one not drinking, asked if I would like to go to church. I did because I didn't want to stay there; plus, I had never been to church before.

Long story short for that night, I got saved. I don't remember much, but I do remember crying so hard, and didn't know why. My Aunt told me it was because Jesus wanted to come into my life. So I know that was my first encounter with Him. (GOD)

2 BOLOGNA & BREAD

After we got back to Tooele, Utah, things got worse. My mother had caught my dad with another woman. She was bound and determined to leave my dad, despite the fact that we had no money and we had no car. She told my older brother she was going to hitchhike to Corpus Christi, Texas with me and my sister, and no one was going to stop her. So he decided to come with us. I am so glad he did! I don't know how we would have made it without him. He was really our guardian and protector.

I don't remember a lot of details. My Mother has passed and so has my brother, so I am going on memory of what I remember; also, what I was told later on in years to follow. I do remember not having much money so we ate a lot of Bologna and bread. We couldn't stay in motels because of money, so we slept in parks and such. My Brother often carried my sister as she was younger than me.

It was hard to catch rides since there were four of us. I remember mama telling me that we would split up in pairs to catch rides. My Brother and I were a pair, and my mother and sister another. One ride she and my sister got was from a trucker who had apparently only wanted sex. She told him to drop her off, because she would rather die fighting than to give into him. He did. (GOD)

Another time we had a Policeman give us a ride. He told us that he wished He could give us a ride all the way, because it broke his heart to see us out on the street, but because of rules he could only give us a ride so far. He took a big chance just letting us in his patrol car.

Anyway, we finally made it close enough to Corpus Christi that my older sister came the rest of the way to get us. (GOD)

3 RELATIONSHIP WITH GOD

My mother and dad made up. He came got us and moved us back to Tooele, where everything started all over again. A few years later, we left my dad again, only this time my mom had a car and a little savings. So, back to Corpus Christi we went. Again, my dad and Mom made up over the telephone, so he moved down to Corpus Christi with us. Of course, nothing had changed; the drinking and fighting continued. By then I was a teenager. I remember walking to the school bus stop, and wondering what it would be like to go back to church like the one in California.

I knew I was a square in Junior High. I tried to be like them, but it just wasn't me. I didn't like the drinking, smoking, cussing, and showing off. It just wasn't me. As a result, I was pretty much a loner in Junior High.

I finally married at seventeen. I quit school and started my own path of drinking and fighting, just like Mom and Dad. I lived in that abuse for twenty seven years.

I really tried to make the marriage work. We had three sons through this marriage. We did both try church. I loved church, but he was so-so with it. I found he liked alcohol and bar life more. This meant I was in and out, in and out of church for twenty seven years. We were constantly fighting, and there was lots of abuse, always lots of physical abuse. I had God in my Heart, but had to choose: either to stay in church and be miserable while he would be the bars; or I could choose to go with him to save our marriage. Or at least that is what I believed.

During this time of on and off going to church, then to the bars, then back to church, I was asked to go to a different kind of church. I went with my niece, and found these people had such a different kind of relationship with God. They acted as if He was really alive! At first I would roll my eyes when someone would say, "The Lord spoke to me this morning…," or, "The Lord told me this or that…" (GOD)

I thought, "Wow! What a crazy bunch of people." Yet they had something I wanted and needed. I went home and definitely wanted to go back, and I did. A lady prayed for me and when I got home and opened my Bible I found that I could actually start understanding it. I didn't know it then, but the blinders had come off my eyes. (GOD)

I witnessed this to my Husband and I later talked to my Brother-in-law. They both decided to go with me the next Sunday. We went to church the next Sunday and both of them got saved and filled with The Holy Spirit. (GOD).

4 TEACHING DADDY TO LOVE

For a few weeks things were perfect. Then, I remember telling God, "If you knew I would love serving you, why did you put me in a dysfunctional home? Why couldn't I have been raised in a Christian home?"

He spoke back and said, "So that you could learn about forgiveness, and your parents are the first."

I sat down and wrote my dad a letter. I wrote about how I forgave him. I wrote about how I understood that he and my mother never knew how to love because love comes from God. If you don't have God, you can't love properly. I told him, "I love you, and I forgive you." (GOD)

I would have loved to have been a fly on the wall as he read this letter. I never knew how he took it, but it was in his drawer when he passed away. I found it when we were cleaning his drawers out. At least, he hadn't thrown it away, so I hoped it had meant something to Him. I really know it did, because I taught my dad to Love. (GOD)

Growing up, he never told anybody he loved them. His

way of telling you that he loved you would be to say, "You know daddy doesn't love you." It wouldn't be in a bad way. It would be in a loving way. I really believe to this day he didn't know how to say, "I love you."

Anyway, since going to church, I have been taught love is all about God. When my Parents would come around, I would always say, "I love you," as they were leaving. My father really got used to hearing this. The reason I know is that one day they came by to visit, but I was really sick. As they were leaving, he turned as they went out the door, and said, "I love you," first. I had taught my dad to say "I love you." (GOD)

I believe there are many more out there that can relate to this story. The world is full of people that do not know how to love, mainly because God is not in the picture.

5 HOME GOING

Books are a divine appointment. It may have taken years for this to come to pass, but at least it didn't die. Excuses are the biggest drawback to getting a book published, saying, "I can't", as well as other excuses.

I pray this book gets published while I am still alive, but it took years for it to be put on paper. I am not getting any younger. However, this is a book that will continue, since it is about my family: my three sons, and their lives. This book may not go on forever on paper, but the testimony of my three sons will go on forever.

Anyway, I know my mother and father after many years of not knowing God they both still made it to Heaven. I know this because both of them had a death bed experience of accepting Jesus into their hearts. Had I not known about the story of the thief on the cross and his last minute experience (Luke 23:39-43), I would not have had the confirmation of my parents' salvation.

At the time of my father's death, my Pastor went to the hospital to see him. He was dying of cancer, and the hospital told us to have him moved to a nursing home since there was no more they could do. My Pastor went to see him the day we were to move him to the nursing home. I was told later after the funeral by my Pastor, J.J. Fox, that he had led Dad to the Lord. (GOD)

He had asked my father if he was ready to go home. My Pastor told me this after the funeral, while my mother was listening. My dad said, "Yes." My mother said, "Of course he was ready to go home! He wanted to come home to be at the lake." My Pastor and I both told Mom, "No. He was ready to go home to be with Jesus."

That was my Dad's experience. My mother's experience was this: a couple of weeks before she passed, she had had an out of body experience. She told me about it. My mother told me she was up above her body, and as she looked down, she saw her body lying on the bed. That body was in a lot of pain, and couldn't breathe. My mother could not get any oxygen in her, even though she had an oxygen machine and two fans on her. She had severe emphysema.

She said she was so peaceful… no pain, no suffering while she was looking down on this lady lying in the bed. She asked me, "What does this mean?" I told her that is what Heaven is like: no pain, no suffering and God was showing her the difference. The day she was actually dying, I ran to my friend's house and asked her to pray for my mom. I couldn't let my mother go. My friend was a wonderful prayer warrior, so I knew she would pray Mom back to life.

But as she prayed, she never mentioned my mother. All she prayed for was for God to comfort me and give me strength. I left there so mad at my friend. I got back to my Mother. She passed on a couple of hours later.

I asked God, "Why didn't my friend pray for my mom? She might have made it!" I heard God say, "She did what I told her to do." (GOD)

I called my Friend, Sister Louie, who has since gone home also, to tell her that Mom had passed on. I told her I was very mad at her for not praying for my mom, and that all she did was pray for me. She said, "Yes I know. I just did what God told me to do. He said your Mother didn't need the prayers, because she was going to be alright. He said that it was you who needed them, because He was going to take her home." (GOD)

It's been many years since this happened, but with tears rolling down my face as I write this, it is like a fresh memory of yesterday. How much God loved my mother, and how much He loved me. (GOD)

Shirley Cochran

6 MIRACLE!

As I write this book, and go back in time to see all the times God was in my life, showing me how much He loved me I realize I could never give Him enough love back. Knowing He gave His Son for me I could never do the same. I say this because my second son, when he was two weeks old, almost died. I had taken him back and forth to the hospital because he kept choking on his formula. I followed every instruction they said: change formulas, change bottles, change nipples, everything to no avail. It got to where he would lose his breath and he would turn blue! I would blow in his face to bring him back.

I finally took him to my doctor and I screamed at him to do something. He got an appointment with a pediatrician and off to Driscoll Children's Hospital we went. They did a 'down the throat test' and immediately found a blocked intestine. He said, "We will operate early in the morning," but that he really didn't know if there was any sense; however, that he would take the chance.

I will never forget that doctor telling me that he might not make it, and did I have any questions? I thought, "What am I supposed to say? What am I supposed to ask? You already told me, he might not make it."

I went to my Pastor's wife, and she prayed for me. I am a Spirit filled Christian. Some of you reading this might not know what being 'slain in the Spirit' is. This is when God's Spirit is so thick, that you can't stand up any more and you fall down, so that He can perform what He needs to do. Sometimes, He will just talk to you and sometimes you will just rest in Him.

To continue my story, my Pastor's wife, Mrs. J.J. Fox, prayed for me and I was slain the Spirit. During this, I was actually standing before God, telling Him, "Please don't take my baby…but if you do, help me to cope with it." I saw myself handing my baby, Keven, to God. God took him from my arms and held him for a minute, then He handed him back to me. I knew before I got up, that my son would be alright.

They operated on him and the doctor came out and said, "Wow, that little boy went through that surgery with flying colors! I am very amazed." (GOD)

Ha! I wasn't. I had a loving God who loved me and loved my son. I knew from that day Keven was a confirmation and a living testimony. I knew that God had a call on his life.

My son was born, June 21, 1977, so whenever this gets

published, you can figure out how many years ago that was. I can't finish his life story because at the moment he is running to and fro from God. The enemy knows he has a calling, and it's been a long, rough road for Keven. As of this moment he is seeking God. (GOD)

Shirley Cochran

7 GOD IS ALWAYS ON THE SCENE

This book is going to be saying that even though years back I didn't know God, He always knew me. He was always on the scene. He was always watching my back. I later learned the scripture Hebrews 13:5, "Let your conduct be without covetousness; be content with such things as you have. For He Himself has said, "I will never leave you nor forsake you." He never did and never will.

Another testimony showing that God was with me and I never knew it was in 1967. I had a sister who took a lot of pills, trying to commit suicide. She went into a coma and died a few days later. I want to show how God was with me and I didn't even know Him.

My sister and I were very close. She was looking for love in all the wrong places. She had four babies, but I would come over every weekend to babysit so she could go out. I was thirteen. Her husband was in the service and never home. When he did come home, there was so much chaos. One weekend, he came home and evidently there was so much chaos, she took a handful of malaria pills, which put her in the hospital, and in a coma.

I got to see her just one time while she was in I.C.U., but I will never forget it. I talked to her as if she could hear me and I believe to this day that she did. I told her that everyone was taking care of her babies and that they would be alright. The family had pitched in to help. Then the most amazing thing happened, and the nurse was standing right there when it happened. While I talked, my sister Barbara made a sound from her throat. The nurse said, "She has never done that. It's as if she hears your voice."

I know she did. I just had that inside feeling. Of course, later on, people told me that anyone that commits suicide automatically goes to hell. How thankful I am that we are not the Judges! This is because I came to the conclusion that if she could reach out to me by that little noise she made, who is to say that she didn't reach out to God before she died. (GOD)

Anyway, years later when my Mother passed away, I was going through some things, and there was the funeral book of my Sister. I opened it, and inside were two poems that had been written by me. I vaguely remembered them, but the point is it had to be God who gave me the inspiration to write them. One of them was how beautiful Heaven was. I didn't know anything about God or Heaven. Now I know that He had always been with me, even if I didn't know it. I believe she made it to Heaven also. I believe He gave me the confirmation by what I had written in those poems. (GOD)

8 NEVER GIVE UP!

I am going on with my testimonies. I don't want this book to be about a sad sob story. I just want people who read this to see what God can do. Even when you don't see the answer right away, never give up. He is our heavenly Father and He loves us so much that He found a way to give us restoration with Him.

Going back to my life, I divorced my husband and decided to go on with my life. I had to find something else besides fighting. I had enough growing up in it and living with it twenty seven years.

I didn't have an education, as I had quit school, so being in the bars at this time, I started working in one. Again, I can look back and see God protecting me. I didn't work in a sleazy type bar; I went to work at the V.F.W. I loved it there, because there were elderly people who loved to come and chat or play Dominoes. (GOD)

I made good money there, so when I learned I could pay

my rent, I divorced my husband. Believe me, I still loved God enough that I paid my tithes to a church I had been attending. They had taught about paying tithes, and I needed God to watch over me. It wasn't always roses either.

Because I was lonely, I also stayed at The V.F.W. a lot after work, and drinking. I left my third son home a lot. He was about thirteen, an age where I should have been in his life. I did not realize that this was a crucial time for him. I believe a lot of the fault is mine for the way he is today. I may have actually passed on rejection to him. I accept it and have asked God to forgive me. I have asked forgiveness from him also, but as of today, there is a lot of bitterness in him. I do believe, one day, he will come around.

There is a lot that is between him and me, not just the way he was raised. In later years things happened, and he had a son taken away from him. By this time, I was remarried and settled down. We loved that little baby, Dylan. Anyway, things happened to the point that Child Protective Services stepped in. We took Dylan in, and are still raising him to this day. Regardless, I believe God will be the testimony of this chapter in my son's life. God is a God of restoration, and forgiveness.

9 PROMISES OF GOD

I want to give some testimonies of how God is always in our lives, whether we realize it at that time or not. In 2005, I had to have a major stomach surgery. I was at this time settled down and going to church. I had been losing blood and really didn't know it. I had gotten very tired and weak and my blood pressure was falling. I had gotten up to go to church and the greeter at the door happened to be a nurse. I showed her my blood pressure notes and she said, "Go to the hospital. Now."

So, I left, went home to get my husband and off we went. I guess I looked a sight, because they took me in right away. I had to have two pints of blood. They found out what was wrong, but wouldn't be doing surgery for a week. The only doctor that knew how to do this kind of surgery was very busy. The reason I am telling this story is I want you to see God in this.

Knowing I had to have surgery, it seemed I went everywhere to find people to pray for me. I was scared and I was looking for someone to tell me everything will be OK and that I wasn't going to die. I went on with the surgery.

On the second day of recovery, a friend of mine from church came to visit. She gave me a daily devotional that had promises from the Bible in it. The very first promise was from Jeremiah 29:11, "For I know the thoughts that I think toward you, says the Lord, thoughts of peace and not of evil, to give you a future and a hope."

Even though the Surgery was over, and I was going to be OK, I was still mad at God about why I didn't have this kind of confirmation before I went into surgery. I asked God, "Why didn't You tell me this before surgery?" His answer was, "Because you went to everyone else for a word instead of coming to ME for 'The Word'!"

Wow, Wow, Wow! I could have crawled under a worms belly, I felt so low. I had been going to church, and had even had a Women's Bible Study in my home; and yet, I still had not trusted God and His Word enough.

I had read and taught His Word, but didn't apply it to myself. Today is different because, His Word is everything! Everything has to be backed up by His Word or I will not accept it. I have had many Bible Studies now, and I encourage everyone to read The Word, to live The Word, and to testify The Word.

10 PROPHETIC WORD

You see, I have found that man lies to us, but "...the Strength of Israel will not lie nor relent. For He is not a man, that He should relent," (1 Sam. 15:29). His Word is Truth. If you are reading this and you know God, you will already know that living a life for Him is not a bed of roses; in fact, things seem to get tougher. But, you will also be able to look back as I have done and see all that He has brought you through. Everybody has a testimony!

I do have another one that I know that I know, (not a misprint) that God was doing everything He could in my earlier years to get me to follow Him.

It was while I was still married to my first husband that I decided to go back to church. I had been in and out, in and out - but my desire was to be "in". I thought I would go back to church, but I was going to go to one where *no one* knew me or about me. We had such a good service on Sunday morning that I wanted to go back Sunday night. Before we could get back that night, my brother appeared on my doorstep, very intoxicated. I asked the Lord, "Why is it that when I want to serve you, alcohol is always knocking on my door?"

I decided to go anyway. I was really down, because it seemed as if I would take one step forward and two back. At the time, I didn't really know the enemy had a lot to do with this. I just blamed God for everything. We went on to church, and that night they had a guest speaker.

Little did I know that God was going to show up! When we got there, I felt as if there were palpitations in my chest. I had never experienced this before. The Speaker started speaking and prophesying. He said, "There is someone here who, every time you take a step forward, the enemy knocks you back two." I knew he was talking about me, but I really couldn't concentrate because my chest was pounding so hard! I thought I was going to have a heart attack. This was my first encounter with God speaking to me alone with a house full of people in church.

He then said, "Turn to Zechariah Chapter 3." I was in such a state, I couldn't do anything but cry, and I mean SOB! So, I just sat there and tried to listen to what he had to say, but he didn't say it. The Lord was speaking it to **me**.

Zechariah 3:1-7

"Then he showed me Joshua the high priest standing before the Angel of the Lord, and Satan standing at his right hand to oppose him. And the Lord said to Satan, "The Lord rebuke you, Satan! The Lord who has chosen Jerusalem rebuke you! Is this not a brand plucked from the fire?"

Now Joshua was clothed with filthy garments, and was standing before the Angel.

Then He answered and spoke to those who stood before Him, saying, "Take away the filthy garments from him." And to him He said, "See, I have removed your iniquity from you, and I will clothe you with rich robes."

And I said, "Let them put a clean turban on his head."

So they put a clean turban on his head, and they put the clothes on him. And the Angel of the Lord stood by.

Then the Angel of the Lord admonished Joshua, saying, "Thus says the Lord of hosts:

'If you will walk in My ways,

And if you will keep My command,

Then you shall also judge My house,

And likewise have charge of My courts;

I will give you places to walk

Among these who stand here."

The Speaker went on to say, "This person that the Lord is speaking to - He says to tell you He has seen you get up out of the mud pit, and when you do, the enemy comes and knocks you back down. The Lord is telling you to keep getting back up. The enemy will never give up, because you have a calling on your life. But, "You are of God, little children, and have overcome them, because He who is in you is greater than he who is in the world," (1 John 4:4).

Oh, what an impact that made on my Life! I guess it was the impact that God really did care for me. Or, maybe, it was then that I realized that if God only sent His Son for one person, it was for me. This was probably the first time I had realized Someone truly loved me. I was special to Somebody. I was learning *Who I Am* and was coming out of *Who Am I?*

11   AARON

I remember one time years ago I had gone to my niece's house to spend the night. We were going to a "special", to hear a special speaker in San Antonio, Texas. Actually, if I remember right, we had three different places to go that weekend. The first thing I remember is going to her own church, and on the wall of her church was the "Aaronic Blessing". I read it and reread it. The Holy Spirit was speaking to me because I couldn't get that "Aaronic Blessing" out of my mind. I kept asking God, "What is it that you want me to get out of this?"

It just wouldn't go away. I kept hearing "Aaron". I pondered all night, *what is it?* The next night we were going to a conference at another church. I could not 'get into' the service because I was so grieved in my spirit. All of a sudden, I heard the Lord say something to me, and the conversation went like this:

Lord: "Do you know who Aaron is?"

Me: Yes

Lord: "Who is he?"

Me: He was Moses' Brother.

Lord: "What did Aaron do for Moses?"

Me: He held up Moses' arms

Lord: "That's what you are, an Aaron, to hold up Leaders' (Pastors') arms."

All of a sudden, the confusion I had been experiencing lifted. Then, for a confirmation, the Pastor of this church said, "I have a scripture for someone here." He said, "Psalm 20:2 – 'May He send you help from the sanctuary,

And strengthen you out of Zion; You will be a Helper. You will be like an Aaron.'"

Well, that filled me with so much joy, I took off running in the church! I didn't care who saw me, or what they thought. All I knew was God had spoken to me.

12 SOMEONE TO HOLD ME

I love going different places to worship, to hear God's word, and hear different speakers. I went to an Assembly of God meeting in Kerrville, Texas to a women's conference. The Woman who spoke was an awesome speaker. I don't remember dates, times, names or anything else, but the point is she told of all the trials she had gone through in her life. She talked about hurts.

I remember thinking, "Wow, and she is a follower of God." By the time she got through speaking, I looked around and saw so many women crying, and I had forgotten about all of my own hurts. She gave the invitation, "If you need prayer for being hurt in your life come to the front."

This conference room held about 500 women, and I truly believe more than half of the room went forward. I couldn't believe it. I was young in the Lord, so at that time I thought that being a Christian meant things would always be better; but, here was more than half of the women in the room going to the front for prayer.

All I could do is go sit with some of them and tell them, "I don't know what you are going through, so I don't know how to pray for you; but I do know how to just hold you while you cry." That's all I wanted to do. God could take care of the inside, but I could hold someone from the outside. Maybe it had been a long time since they had been held. I had known what that was like, not having someone to hold me.

13 THE WILDERNESS

This chapter is about 'the wilderness'. The wilderness is a very lonely place to go through and we all have to go through it sometime or another. When you go through it, you will start asking questions like:

"What did I do wrong Lord?"

"What did I do to deserve this?"

"Are you mad at me Lord?" and especially, "Where did you go?"

Then, if you know the Word, you will start picking at the scriptures:

"Lord, You said You will never leave me nor forsake me."

"You said You weren't a respector of persons. Why doesn't (he/she) ever go through anything?"

I always was condemning myself with this one, "Well, what you sow is what you reap. I guess I wasn't sowing good things."

Then, as you do get a little wiser from going through these quiet times in the wilderness, not hearing from God, you start to learn some things to help you. You even receive some blessings after going through the wilderness, and find out you may be a few more steps closer to God.

And even though we still go through trials and tribulations, we finally learn the main important thing: that we didn't go through them alone, even if it felt like we did.

Now, we can turn those scriptures around that He doesn't ever leave us or forsake us. He is still right where He was when we were going through the wilderness, and that He is still in our heart…right where He always was. It's just that now, He is letting us do some walking on our own.

To learn to rely on His Word instead of Him leading us by the Hand all the time.

We all have a destination. In today's times, if we want to get from Dallas to Florida, we can go hop a Plane and get there faster than if we drive. But years back, if you had to drive, you had to travel roads to get from *Point A* to *Point B*. Not all those roads were smooth. They might have been rocky, rainy, windy, etc. We all have a destination and sometimes we have to go through a wilderness to get there.

I learned that by going through rough times that we are not supposed to look at what we're going through; rather, we're to look at where it's taking us.

Remember, sometimes, we cry for shoes, until we find a

man with no feet. After you came out of the wilderness, you found out it wasn't so bad, right? Well, just hang on, because you might see another one in front of you!

From Who Am I? to Who I AM!

14 I LOVE YOU!

I am not sure if this is the last chapter or not, but if it is, so be it. If it's not, then to God be the glory.

In my sleep one night, I kept getting this phrase, "Don't ever give up on telling your loved ones that you love them. Don't ever get slack in telling the Father that you love Him." I kept hearing this so much through the night. I finally realized that I had become slack and lazy about telling my family, "I love you."

I thought about my oldest sister, who has passed on. She told me about her husband's death. He had left the house for work one day and his car had broken down. Long story short, another car came by and ran into him and killed him. She had never thought that it would be the last time they would see each other when they said goodbye earlier that morning.

The Bible says we are like flowers - here one day, gone the next. We take it for granted that things will be ok and then, Boom!

Always tell your children that you love them. Tell your parents, your loved ones, your friends, your sisters and brothers in Christ. Always pray and tell the Father that you love Him. Thank Him for what He has done for us, by sending His own Son to die for me and for You. Thank Jesus for shedding His blood for me and for you. Tell Him how much you love Him. Tell Holy Spirit how much you love Him for being our teacher, guide and comforter.

After all, He is the God of I Am, and not the God of I Was!

God Bless

15   WHO I AM

OK. I am ready to finalize this.

Finishing up the book, I have come across not just my new identity, but others' as well. I have been ministering to a wonderful establishment called, "Alabaster". These are ladies who have come through some heavy and rough times of addictions themselves, but they have also found freedom in Jesus Christ. After all, "We have all sinned and fallen short of the glory of God," (Romans 3:23).

My Bible also tells me, in Romans 5:20, "Moreover the law entered that the offense might abound. But where sin abounded, grace abounded much more."

Give someone a hug today and tell them you love them and God loves them so much that He gave His only begotten Son for them.

After all, we are all a diamond in the rough, coming from a chunk of coal.

Psalm 45:1, "My heart is overflowing with a good theme; I recite my composition concerning the King; My tongue *is* the pen of a ready writer."

16 DREAM OF THE MULTI COLORED HENS

I had a dream and it was so real, I know it came from The Lord. I have my own interpretation, but you're welcome to see it as you do.

I was standing at my front door looking out of the screen door. Everything was in the shade of gray. It was my property, with my fence up front and my gate and trees, everything was just like it is right now if I looked out my front door. Like I said, everything was in gray, except outside my gate in the driveway there were two hens, and they were the most incredibly beautiful hens. I want to say more than I have ever seen, except there are no real hens that can be this beautiful. They were multi colored. No color on them was there twice.

I looked up different things in dream books and this is what I got:

The hens are protectors. They were protecting my property. The multiple colors were God's colors, multifaceted. Multifaceted could mean His Glory, multifaceted could mean the brilliance of a diamond. If you turn a true diamond you will never see the same color twice.

We have hens on our property. The Lord said, "I had to have everything in gray so that you would notice the hens better in color. Had I left them in gray, the dream wouldn't have meant much. But I had to make you look at what I really wanted you to see: the multi-colored hens."

My niece gave me this interpretation, and since then, I believe I have seen some of the facets of His Glory, just like the diamond. I'm inserting this in my book since my book is all about us coming from the shade of gray to His multi-colored Glory.

CONCLUSION: GOD'S PLAN

If God can change a pebble into a pearl, a worm into a butterfly, an acorn into an oak tree, and a chunk of coal into a diamond, look at what He can do for us.

It comes from pressure and maturity.

My prayer is you will see how God has a plan for your life.

From Who Am I? to Who I AM!

ABOUT THE AUTHOR

Shirley Abbott Cochran is a wife, mother, grandmother, great grandmother and has lots of sisters and brothers in Christ.

She came from a dysfunctional family, so she knows what it is to be broken and hurt. She loves to teach the word and the hope it brings.

Her prayer is this book reaches out to the hurting and broken; to the drug addicts, alcoholics, and the abused.

After all, this is whom Jesus came for, for whom He died and bled.

www.ingramcontent.com/pod-product-compliance
Lightning Source LLC
Chambersburg PA
CBHW071741020426
42331CB00008B/2128